CAT POEMS

SELECTED BY
Myra Cohn Livingston

ILLUSTRATED BY
Trina Schart Hyman

OXFORD UNIVERSITY PRESS

To our friend
LLOYD ALEXANDER
with love
M.C.L. & T.S.H.

Oxford University Press, Walton Street, Oxford OX2 6DP

Oxford   New York
Athens   Auckland   Bangkok   Bombay
Calcutta   Cape Town   Dar es Salaam   Delhi
Florence   Hong Kong   Istanbul   Karachi
Kuala Lumpur   Madras   Madrid   Melbourne
Mexico City   Nairobi   Paris   Singapore
Taipei   Tokyo   Toronto

and associated companies in
Berlin   Ibadan

Oxford is a trade mark of Oxford University Press

Text copyright © 1987 by Myra Cohn Livingston
Illustrations copyright © 1987 by Trina Schart Hyman
First published by Holiday House, New York

First published in the UK by Oxford University Press 1989
First published in paperback 1994
Reprinted 1995

British Library Cataloguing in Publication Data
Cat poems
1. Children's poetry in English.
Special subjects: Animals - Anthologies
I. Livingston, Myra Cohn II Hyman,
Trina Schart
821'.008'036

ISBN 0-19-276081-5 (hardback)
ISBN 0-19-276131-5 (paperbarck)

Printed in Hong Kong

CONTENTS

CAT'S TONGUE

Cat's tongue,
Cat's tongue,
Pink as clover.

Cat's tongue,
Cat's tongue,
Wash all over.

Lick your paws,
Lick your face,
The back of your neck
And every place.

Lick your whiskers,
Smooth your fur,
Prick up your ears
And purr, purr, purr.

Cat's tongue,
Cat's tongue,
Pink as clover.

Cat's tongue,
Cat's tongue,
Clean all over.

EVE MERRIAM

CATNIP

Musky mint,
A mousy green,
Not much of a
Smell, at that—

And yet it turns
Tabby or Tom
To a fool, a
Lunatic acrobat.

Then what is its
Magic, hidden from
All but the wise
Nose of the cat?

VALERIE WORTH

THE CAT HEARD THE CAT-BIRD

One day, a fine day, a high-flying-sky day,
A cat-bird, a fat bird, a fine fat cat-bird
Was sitting and singing on a stump by the highway.
Just sitting. And singing. Just that. But a cat heard.

A thin cat, a grin-cat, a long thin grin-cat
Came creeping the sly way by the highway to the stump.
"O cat-bird, the cat heard! O cat-bird scat!
The grin-cat is creeping! He's going to jump!"

—One day, a fine day, a high-flying-sky day
A fat cat, yes, that cat we met as a thin cat
Was napping, cat-napping, on a stump by the highway,
And even in his sleep you could see he was a grin-cat.

Why was he grinning? —He must have had a dream.
What made him fat? —A pan full of cream.
What about the cat-bird? —What bird, dear?
I don't see any cat-bird here.

JOHN CIARDI

CAT

Cat!
Scat!
Atter her, atter her,
Sleeky flatterer,
Spitfire chatterer,
Scatter her, scatter her
 Off her mat!
 Wuff!
 Wuff!
 Treat her rough!
Git her, git her,
Whiskery spitter!
Catch her, catch her,
Green-eyed scratcher!
 Slathery
 Slithery
 Hisser,
 Don't miss her!
Run till you're dithery,
 Hithery
 Thithery!
 Pftts! pftts!
 How she spits!
 Spitch! spatch!
 Can't she scratch!

Scritching the bark
Of the sycamore-tree,
She's reached her ark
And's hissing at me
   Pfitts! pfitts!
   Wuff! wuff!
    Scat,
    Cat!
    That's
    That!

ELEANOR FARJEON

CATSNEST

Tread.

Tread.

Our cat treads my bed,
Pushing my spread to a heap for his sleep,
Punching sheets, stretching his tailbone up tall—
That it's me underneath doesn't matter at all—

And at last when he's hollowed a hollow he likes
He fits down inside it and, satisfied, purrs
Until Grandmother comes in to turn out my light
And to tell me good night. Then he angrily stirs
And he fluffs up gigantic and glowers, to say:
Well, I did all that digging—why shouldn't *I stay?*

X. J. KENNEDY

MY CAT, ROBIN HOOD

My cat is a tough hood.
He slurps my milk and cereal,
licks my apples and my cookies,
and scratches me
when he's in no mood to play.
He steals my socks
and my baseball cap
and thinks our sofa
is a toy for ripping.

But my cat is also
like a gentle Robin Bird.
He tickles me with his soft tail
and purrs and winks
when I scratch his belly.
He opens the dark
with his bright eyes,
and he sleeps warmly
at my feet on winter nights.

EMANUEL DI PASQUALE

CATALOG

Cats sleep fat and walk thin.
Cats, when they sleep, slump;
When they wake, pull in——
And where the plump's been
There's skin.
Cats walk thin.

Cats wait in a lump,
Jump in a streak.
Cats, when they jump, are sleek
As a grape slipping its skin——
They have technique.
Oh, cats don't creak.
They sneak.

Cats sleep fat.
They spread comfort beneath them
Like a good mat,
As if they picked the place
And then sat.
You walk around one
As if he were the City Hall
After that.

If male,
A cat is apt to sing upon a major scale:
This concert is for everybody, this
Is wholesale.
For a baton, he wields a tail.

(He is also found,
When happy to resound
With an enclosed and private sound.)

A cat condenses.
He pulls in his tail to go under bridges,
And himself to go under fences.
Cats fit
In any size box or kit;
And if a large pumpkin grew under one,
He could arch over it.

When everyone else is just ready to go out,
The cat is just ready to come in.
He's not where he's been.
Cats sleep fat and walk thin.

ROSALIE MOORE

16

MISS TIBBLES

Miss Tibbles is my kitten; white
as day she is and black as night.

She moves in little gusts and breezes
sharp and sudden as a sneeze is.

At hunting Tibbles has no match.
How I like to see her catch

moth or beetle, two a penny,
and feast until there isn't any!

Sometimes I like her calm, unwild,
gentle as a sleeping child,

and wonder as she lies, a fur ring,
curled upon my lap, unstirring,—
is it me or Tibbles purring?

IAN SERRAILLIER

THE SONG OF THE JELLICLES

Jellicle Cats come out tonight,
Jellicle Cats come one come all:
The Jellicle Moon is shining bright——
Jellicles come to the Jellicle Ball.

Jellicle Cats are black and white,
Jellicle Cats are rather small;
Jellicle Cats are merry and bright,
And pleasant to hear when they caterwaul.
Jellicle Cats have cheerful faces,
Jellicle Cats have bright black eyes;
They like to practise their airs and graces
And wait for the Jellicle Moon to rise.

Jellicle Cats develop slowly,
Jellicle Cats are not too big;
Jellicle Cats are roly-poly,
They know how to dance a gavotte and a jig.
Until the Jellicle Moon appears
They make their toilette and take their repose:
Jellicles wash behind their ears,
Jellicles dry between their toes.

Jellicle Cats are white and black,
Jellicle Cats are of moderate size;
Jellicles jump like a jumping-jack,
Jellicle Cats have moonlit eyes.
They're quiet enough in the morning hours,
They're quiet enough in the afternoon,
Reserving their terpsichorean powers
To dance by the light of the Jellicle Moon.

Jellicle Cats are black and white,
Jellicle Cats (as I said) are small;
If it happens to be a stormy night
They will practise a caper or two in the hall.
If it happens the sun is shining bright
You would say they had nothing to do at all:
They are resting and saving themselves to be right
For the Jellicle Moon and the Jellicle Ball.

T. S. ELIOT

THE OPEN DOOR

Out of the dark
to the sill of the door
lay the snow in a long
unruffled floor,
and the lamplight fell
narrow and thin
a carpet unrolled
for the cat to walk in.
Slowly, smoothly,
black as the night,
with paws unseen
(white upon white)
like a queen who walks
down a corridor
the black cat paced
that cold smooth floor,
and left behind her,
bead upon bead,
the track of small feet
like dark fern seed.

ELIZABETH COATSWORTH

MARMALADE LOST

Her honey fur pointed down her back
to her almost lady hips.

She only showed her claws for love,
was particular about her paws,

and never first to dinner.
Hated rain, liked beds,

was clever climbing down a tree,
the hardest part for kittens.

Did a yen for wandering tempt her,
lured by a hedge or a tom?

Did a truck betray her?
For ten days I've prayed her home,

running like a little bell at dusk,
bouncing like a ballerina,

dainty at my opening door.

RUTH WHITMAN

AMANDA

Amanda was an alley cat.
Not fluffy,
she was dusty, scarred and lean.
She lived,
like other alley cats,
behind old walls,
beneath parked cars.
She did not know that grass was green.
She did not know the night had stars,
just streetlights
taxi cabs
more cars
to hide beneath
to dodge between.
She hunted rats.
She ran from man.
And loved
(as much as she loved anything at all)
a garbage can.

KARLA KUSKIN

22

A TOMCAT IS

Nightwatchman of corners
Caretaker of naps
Leg-wrestler of pillows
Depresser of laps

A master at whining
And dining on mouse
Designer of shadows
That hide in the house.

The bird-watching bandit
On needle-point claws
The chief of detectives
On marshmallow paws

A crafty yarn-spinner
A stringer high-strung
A handlebar mustache
A sandpaper tongue

The dude in the alley
The duke of the couch
Affectionate fellow
Occasional grouch

J. PATRICK LEWIS

CAT & THE WEATHER

Cat takes a look at the weather:
snow;
puts a paw on the sill;
his perch is piled, is a pillow.

Shape of his pad appears:
will it dig? No,
not like sand,
like his fur almost.

But licked, not liked:
too cold.
Insects are flying, fainting down.
He'll try

to bat one against the pane.
They have no body and no buzz,
and now his feet are wet;
it's a puzzle.

24

Shakes each leg,
then shakes his skin
to get the white flies off;
looks for his tail,

tells it to come on in
by the radiator.
World's turned queer
somehow: all white,

no smell. Well, here
inside it's still familiar.
He'll go to sleep until
it puts itself right.

MAY SWENSON

Sing, sing, what shall I sing?
The cat's run away with the pudding string:
Do, do, what shall I do?
The cat has bitten it quite in two!

Nursery Rhyme

CAT: CHRISTMAS

There's always
A ball or
A mouse,

Fondly
Packaged
And given,

Received
With gracious
Attention:

But the
Real success
Is the ribbon.

VALERIE WORTH

CAT

By the fire, like drifting reddish goldfish,
the cat dozed, curled within itself.
If, by mischance, I were to stir,
the cat might change to something else.

The spinning-wheel of ancient magic
must never be allowed to stick:
and changing itself into a princess
is, for the cat, a minor trick.

JEAN COCTEAU
Translated by Alastair Reid

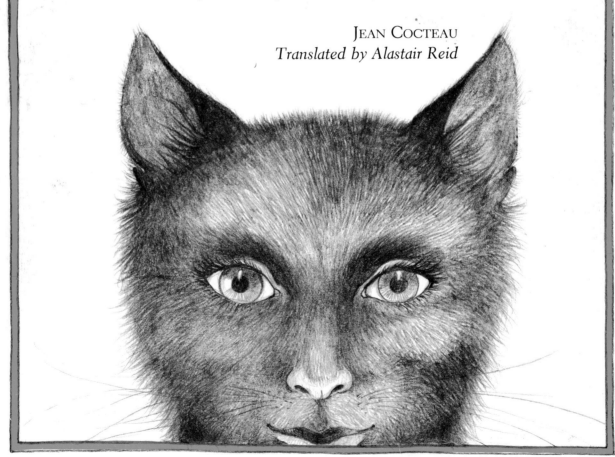

MOON

I have a white cat whose name is Moon;
He eats catfish from a wooden spoon,
And sleeps till five each afternoon.

Moon goes out when the moon is bright
And sycamore trees are spotted white
To sit and stare in the dead of night.

Beyond still water cries a loon,
Through mulberry leaves peers a wild baboon
And in Moon's eyes I see the moon.

WILLIAM JAY SMITH

IN AUGUST ONCE

In August once
just Charlie and the cat
driving to the island
in a small white car.
And then
when they were neither here nor there,
stopping for gas
along the road in Maine,
Charlie looked in to check the cat
pat the black
scratch an ear
and looked again.

In August
going down a country road
at sixty per
our much loved cat, dear Ace,
jumped out the window,
left hand rear,
confused perhaps
or simply filled with fear
of driving.
Charlie searched and searched for her
but she was gone for good.
He walked the rutted, wooded roads
calling her name,
miles back
and years ago
in August. Once.

We've had some other cats since then.
They haven't been the same.

KARLA KUSKIN

ACKNOWLEDGMENTS

Grateful acknowledgment is made to the following poets, whose work was especially commissioned for this book:

Emanuel di Pasquale for "My Cat, Robin Hood." Copyright © 1987 by Emanuel di Pasquale.

Karla Kuskin for "Amanda" and "In August Once." Copyright © 1987 by Karla Kuskin.

J. Patrick Lewis for "A Tomcat Is." Copyright © 1987 by J. Patrick Lewis.

Valerie Worth for "Cat: Christmas" and "Catnip." Copyright © 1987 by Valerie Worth.

Grateful acknowledgment is also made for the following reprints:

Atheneum Publishers, Inc. for "Catsnest" by X. J. Kennedy from *The Forgetful Wishing Well.* Copyright © 1985 by X. J. Kennedy. (A Margaret K. McElderry Book.) Reprinted with the permission of Atheneum, Inc.

Delacorte Press for "Moon" excerpted from the book *Laughing Time* by William Jay Smith. Copyright © 1953, 1955, 1956, 1957, 1959, 1968, 1974, 1977, 1980 by William Jay Smith. Reprinted by permission of Delacorte Press/Seymour Lawrence.

Harcourt Brace Jovanovich, Inc. and Faber and Faber Ltd. for "The Song of the Jellicles" by T. S. Eliot from *Old Possum's Book of Practical Cats* by T. S. Eliot. Copyright 1939 by T. S. Eliot; renewed 1967 by Esme Valerie Eliot. Reprinted by permission of Harcourt Brace Jovanovich, Inc.

Harper & Row, Publishers, Inc. for "Cat" from Eleanor Farjeon's *Poems for Children* (J. B. Lippincott). Copyright 1938, renewed 1966 by Eleanor Farjeon. Reprinted by permission of Harper & Row, Publishers, Inc.

Houghton Mifflin Company for "The Cat Heard the Cat-Bird" in *I Met a Man* by John Ciardi. Copyright © 1961 by John Ciardi. Reprinted by permission of Houghton Mifflin Company.

Seymour Lawrence for "Cat" by Jean Cocteau, translated by Alastair Reid, excerpted from *Irene's Pennywhistle,* first published in Wake. Copyright © 1953, Wake Editions. Reprinted by permission of Wake Editions, Seymour Lawrence, sole owner.

Macmillan Publishing Company for "The Open Door" by Elizabeth Coatsworth from *Away Goes Sally* by Elizabeth Coatsworth. Copyright 1934 by Macmillan Publishing Company, renewed 1962 by Elizabeth Coatsworth Beston.

William Morrow & Co. for "Cat's Tongue" from *Blackberry Ink* by Eve Merriam. Copyright © 1985 by Eve Merriam. Reprinted by permission of Marian Reiner for the author.

The New Yorker for "Catalog" by Rosalie Moore. Reprinted by permission; © 1940, 1968 The New Yorker Magazine, Inc.

Ian Serraillier for "Miss Tibbles" from *The Monster Horse* published by Oxford University Press. Copyright © 1950 by Ian Serraillier, and Oxford University Press.

May Swenson for "Cat & the Weather" from *To Mix with Time, New & Selected Poems.* Copyright © 1963 by May Swenson. Reprinted by permission of the author.

Ruth Whitman for "Marmalade Lost" from *A Celebration of Cats,* ed. Jean Burden. Copyright © 1974. Reprinted by permission of the author.